TABLE OF CONTE

BLACKBIRD

Words and Music by JOHN LENNON and
PAUL McCARTNEY

YOUR SONG

Words and Music by ELTON JOHN
and BERNIE TAUPIN

SET FIRE TO THE RAIN

Words & Music by Fraser Smith & Adele Adkins

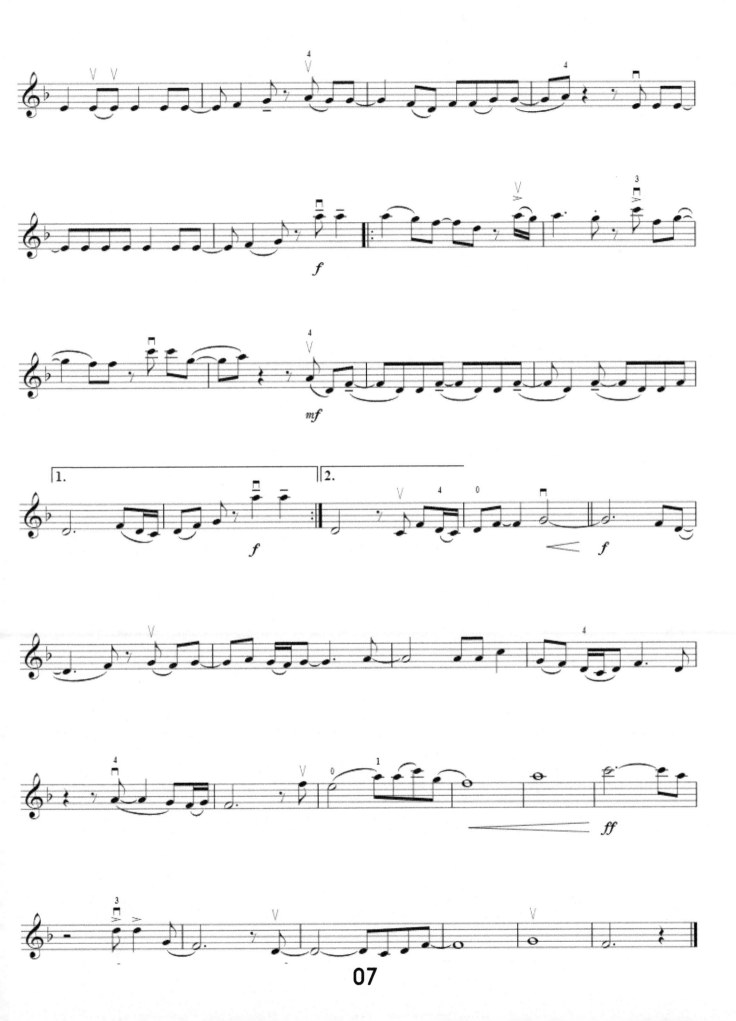

Quasi rubato

p dolce

mp

LIFE ON MARS?

Words & Music by David Bowie

10

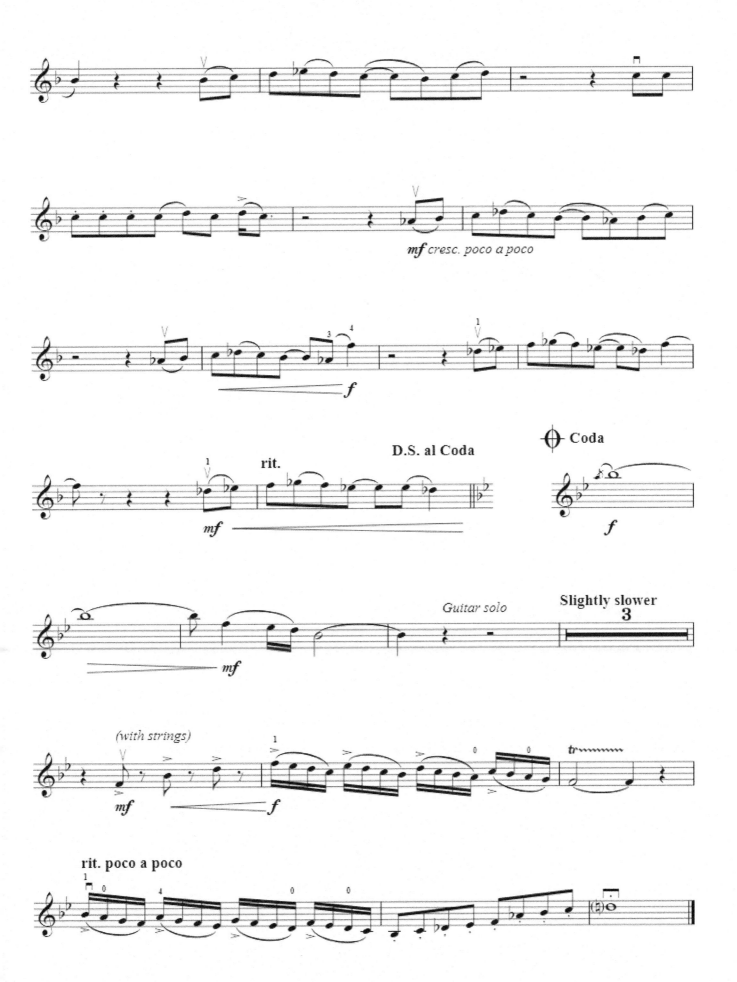

MULL OF KINTYRE

Words & Music by Paul McCartney & Denny Laine

Rather slow, swing

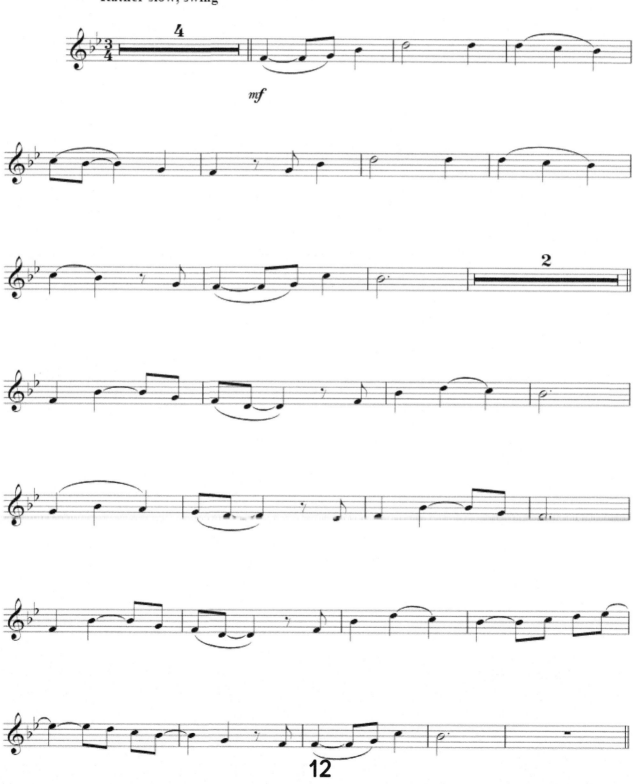

13

FIX YOU

Words & Music by Guy Berryman, Chris Martin,
Jon Buckland & Will Champion

15

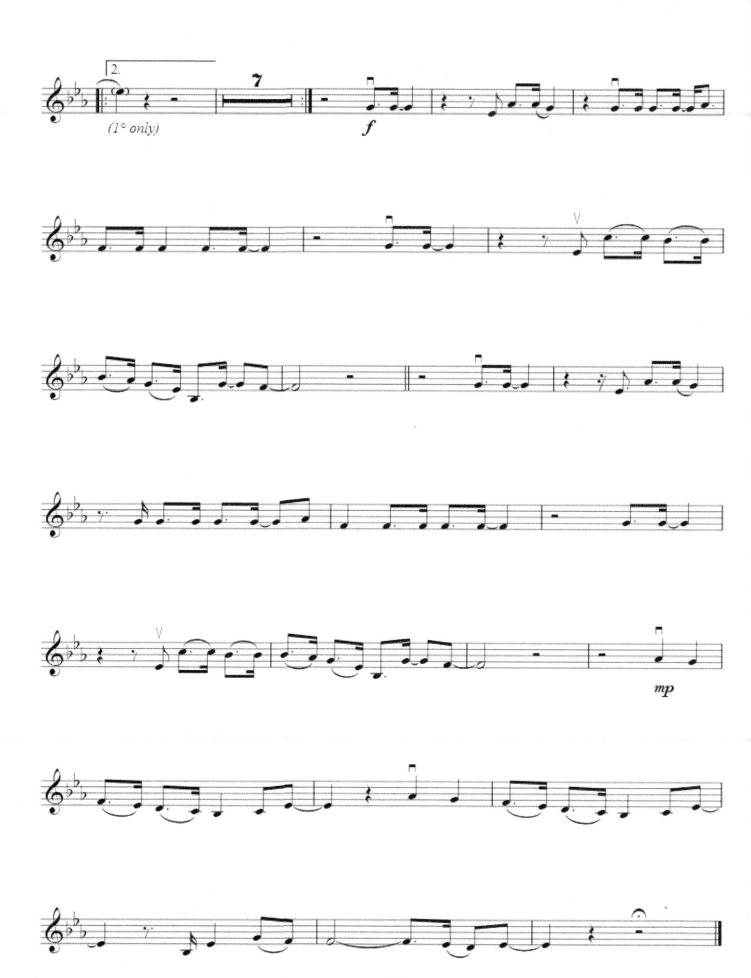

HALLELUJAH

Words & Music by Leonard Cohen

rit.

mp

APOLOGIZE

Words & Music by Ryan Tedder

RUN

Words & Music by Gary Lightbody, Jonathan Quinn, Mark
McClelland, Nathan Connolly & Iain Archer

rit.

YELLOW

Words & Music by Guy Berryman, Chris
Martin, Jon Buckland & Will Champion

26

27

THE SCIENTIST

Words & Music by Guy Berryman, Chris Martin, Jon
Buckland & Will Champion

29

30

BRIDGE OVER TROUBLED WATER

Words & Music by Paul Simon

32

MAKE YOU FEEL MY LOVE

Words & Music by Bob Dylan

34

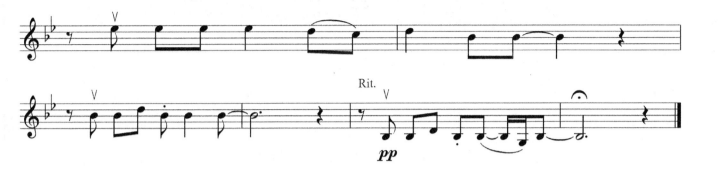

DON'T STOP BELIEVIN'

Words & Music by Steve Perry, Neal Schon
& Jonathan Cain

To Coda

38

D.S. al Coda

Coda

(guitar solo)

YOU RAISE ME UP

Words & Music by Brendan Graham &
Rolf Løvland

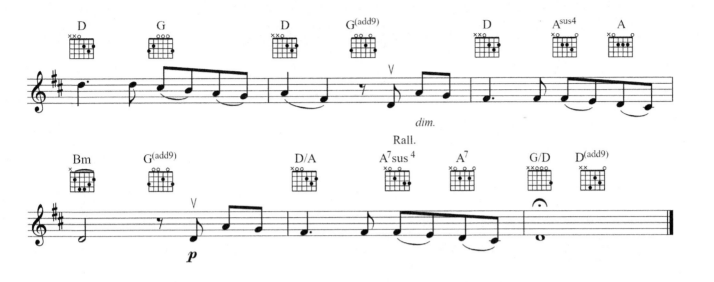

43

BORN TO DIE

Words & Music by Elizabeth Grant &
Justin Parker

45

46

STAY

Words & Music by Justin Parker & Mikky Ekko

47

FIELDS OF GOLD

Words & Music by Sting

STAND BY ME

Words and Music by JERRY LEIBER, MIKE
STOLLER and BEN E. KING

BLESS THE BROKEN ROAD

Words and Music by MARCUS HUMMON, BOBBY
BOYD and JEFF HANNA

THE DEVIL WENT DOWN TO GEORGIA

Words and Music by CHARLIE DANIELS, JOHN THOMAS CRAIN, JR.,
WILLIAM JOEL DiGREGORIO, FRED LAROY EDWARDS, CHARLES
FRED HAYWARD and JAMES WAINWRIGHT MARSHALL

To Coda

1, 2.

3.

D.S. al Coda

TAKE ME HOME, COUNTRY ROADS

Words and Music by JOHN DENVER, BILL
DANOFF and TAFFY NIVERT

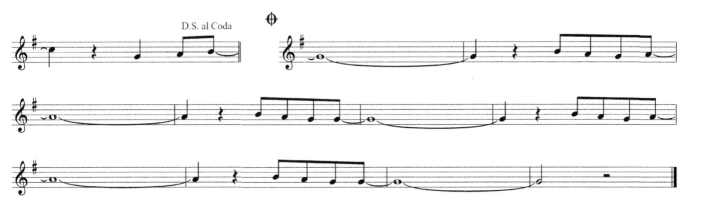

THE SOUND OF SILENCE

Words and Music by PAUL SIMON

DUST IN THE WIND

Words and Music by
KERRY LIVGRE

FIREWORK

Words and Music by KATY PERRY, MIKKEL ERIKSEN, TOR ERIK HERMANSEN,
ESTHER DEAN and SANDY WILHELM

LET IT GO

Music and Lyrics by KRISTEN ANDERSON-LOPEZ and ROBERT LOPEZ

D.S. al Fine

BAD DAY

Words and Music by DANIEL POWTER

SOMEONE LIKE YOU

Words & Music by Adele Adkins & Daniel Wilson

LET HER GO

Words and Music by MICHAEL DAVID ROSENBERG

PERFECT

Words and Music by ED SHEERAN

SEE YOU AGAIN

Words and Music by CAMERON THOMAZ, CHARLIE PUTH, JUSTIN FRANKS
and ANDREW CEDAR

A THOUSAND YEARS

Words and Music by DAVID HODGES and CHRISTINA PERRI

WHAT A WONDERFUL WORLD

Words & Music by George Weiss & Bob Thiele

Violin

IMAGINE

Words and Music by JOHN LENNON

HERE COMES THE SUN

Words and Music by GEORGE HARRISON

HO HEY

Words and Music by JEREMY FRAITES and WESLEY SCHULTZ

VIVA LA VIDA

Words and Music by GUY BERRYMAN, JON BUCKLAND, WILL CHAMPION and CHRIS
MARTIN

BRAVE

Words and Music by SARA BAREILLES and JACK ANTONOFF

D.S. al Coda

FIGHT SONG

Words and Music by RACHEL PLATTEN and DAVE BASSETT

FEEL IT STILL

Words and Music by JOHN GOURLEY, ZACH CAROTHERS, JASON SECHRIST, ERIC HOWK, KYLE O'QUIN,
BRIAN HOLLAND, FREDDIE GORMAN, GEORGIA DOBBINS, ROBERT BATEMAN, WILLIAM
GARRETT, JOHN HILL and ASA TACCONE

CITY OF STARS

Music by JUSTIN HURWITZ
Lyrics by BENJ PASEK & JUSTIN PAUL

A SKY FULL OF STARS

Words & Music by Guy Berryman, Jonathan Buckland,
William Champion, Christopher Martin & Tim Bergling

EVERMORE

Music by ALAN MENKEN
Lyrics by TIM RICE

CHASING CARS

Words and Music by GARY LIGHTBODY, TOM SIMPSON, PAUL WILSON,
JONATHAN QUINN and NATHAN CONNOLLY

WHAT MAKES YOU BEAUTIFUL

Words and Music by SAVAN KOTECHA, RAMI YACOUB and CARL FALK

KISS FROM A ROSE

Words & Music by Seal

Smoothly, with a lilt ♩ = 132

oboe cue

mp dolce

p   *cresc.*

mp   *f espress.*

Coda

oboe cue

mf legato

mf dolce

molto cresc.   *f*

mp dolce

f espress.

LAST CHRISTMAS

Words & Music by George Michael

very next day you gave it a - way. ___ This year ___ to

save me from tears I'll give it to some - one spe - cial.

Last Christ - mas I gave you my heart, but the ve - ry next day you

gave it a - way. ___ This year ___ to save me from tears I'll

give it to some - one spe - cial.

ALL OF ME

Words & Music by John Legend & Tobias Gad

BOHEMIAN RHAPSODY

Words and Music by
FREDDIE MERCURY

BOULEVARD OF BROKEN DREAMS

Words by Billie Joe
Music by Green Day
Arranged by Lindsey Stirling

MAMMA MIA

Words & Music by Benny Andersson, Stig Anderson
& Björn Ulvaeus

Repeat and fade

111

MAD WORLD

Words & Music by Roland Orzabal

114

CARELESS WHISPER

Words & Music by George Michael & Andrew Ridgeley

ff *more punchy*

Repeat to fade

I WILL ALWAYS LOVE YOU

Words & Music by Dolly Parton

rit.

mp

A tempo

electric piano cue

mp dolce

molto rit.

Much slower

p

GRENADE

Words & Music by Philip Lawrence, Peter Hernandez,Christopher
Brown, Ari Levine, Claude Kelly & Andrew Wyatt

JAR OF HEARTS

Words & Music by Christina Perri, Drew
Lawrence & Barrett Yeretsian

125

BAD ROMANCE

Words & Music by Stefani
Germanotta & RedOne

FIREFLIES

Words & Music by Adam Young

MOON RIVER

Words by JOHNNY MERCER
Music by HENRY MANCINI

100 YEARS

Words and Music by JOHN ONDRASIK

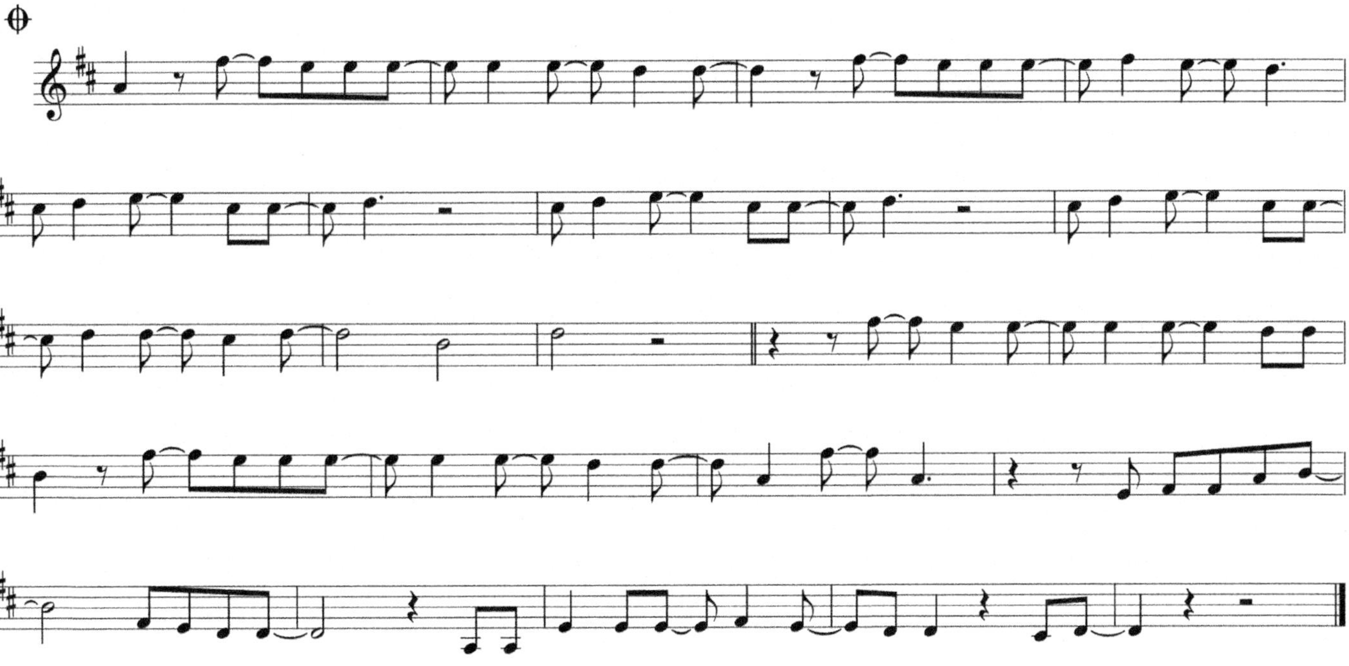

Printed in Great Britain
by Amazon

33325050R00077